Who Gathered
And Whispered
Behind Me

Albert Goldbarth

Who Gathered
And Whispered
Behind Me

L'Epervier Press

Acknowledgments

These poems have appeared, in whole or in part, in the following journals — and grateful thanks is made to their editors: *Bits, Carolina Quarterly, Cutbank, The Falcon.*

The prose section ending "The Window Is An Almanach" is closely patterned after a section of Robert Jeffries' book for children, *Wood Magic.*

Library of Congress Cataloging in Publication Data
Goldbarth, Albert.
    Who gathered and whispered behind me.
    CONTENTS: The window is an almanach. — The family business. — Flag/mole/pygmy/stars/ & iran.
    I. Title.
PS3557.0354W5   811'.54   80-21309
ISBN 0-934332-31-2
ISBN 0-934332-27-4 (pbk.)

Cover illustration of Chartres rose window from Villard d'Honnecourt's Notebook, from *Chartres* by Titus Burckhardt.

Book design by Bridget Culligan
Typesetting by Christopher C. Young,
Seattle, Washington
Printing by Commercial Printing Company,
Fort Collins, Colorado

L'Epervier Press books are available at your local bookstore, or may be ordered from Small Press Distribution, 1784 Shattuck Avenue, Berkeley, California 94709.

for
my sister, Livia

Now Mr. Gaul knew perfectly well that he
had no right to betray their friend Mag-
nus; and yet he also knew that it was im-
portant to help this daughter to forget his
unlucky mention of her father. Such were
the convoluted responsibilities of human
conversation.

— John Cowper Powys

CONTENTS

The Window Is An Almanach

"Let there be light, and there was light."
To whatsoever the word *vayehi* (and there
was) is applied, that thing is in this world
and in the world to come.

— *The Zohar*

Stained glass is easy. The same thing
happens in a cathedral or a synagogue: a
mystical thing passes through the glass.

— Marc Chagall

.

I'm five, she's fifty-five, and there's no way
my ear in the darkness can hold her voice

in the darkness. I only know when Grandma returns
from somewhere called *The Hop-sital*, there are sounds in her room

that Mommy makes from a place in the throat I've never heard
opened, and Daddy's drone like a stroke down the dog's glossy head

to calm a frenzy, and Grandma: *Oy*, drawn long, *I'm
not no vooman no more*, which is a language

I can't understand though I shake at its elocution. And
one day, later, it will seem my whole life was a studying

that vocabulary and its translation.

*

So now you're Pain's prick.
So this is Pain's self-abuse.

So now that gymnast Pain self-fellates
and you're in its mouth, again, so

this is Pain's soliloquy.

A private speech, nobody understands or
can or will, what Pain is saying, saying

with you on its tongue, in the deep place. Only
your face may show it. Only your face, and

vaguely, as a window shows its store

in a ghetto neighborhood: through grime,
through motley cartons stacked in skelter, a

dull cat curled for the sun, and three glass webs
where rocks hit. Once, as a child, you stood here

fixed to the day while someone in the store beyond
your seeing, grieved and the words meant nothing

— thick as Yiddish, peppered as Puerto Rican,
as strange. Its phlegms and flutings

made their sense till the rest of the world spoke gibberish.
This was long ago, a sign said 5 cents

in heavy black crayon. And there were large words

painted, shaky, red on the window, GROCERY STORE or
SHOES REPAIRED or MASSAGE PARLOR, who knew?

but you

in your polyglot moment, you could read it
back for all of us: IN ANOTHER TIME, IN ANOTHER
        COUNTRY

— you faltered (it was new to you) but then kept on —
THIS COULD BE YOUR STORE.

Night; the
child tucked in. And the world,
once the eyes' own pinpoint, vestigial
zodiacs fade, refuses sight. Looking
can't land. The world is total
float-in-dark, *sans* direction,
sans surface, *sans* depth
                              but
for the quarter-inch
bar of glow
from the stay-awake-world, where it manifests
solidity and command
between the invisible door and invisible floor. It
conducts. It's the universal standard
weight and measure, and
brands night's hide. And the boy
could slip from bed now, and lift this
heavy, overspilling
gold rod — and sign, and
endorse, the blankness . . .

*

. . . The blind man, tapping
black with cane — whose sight
is touch and this
single antenna.

Suppose the child's tucked in the rank, littered, slat-bed
darkness of ghetto Russia. "My sweet stars;
they accompany me to school and wait for me on the street
till I return." Light calls him. He sleeps in the loft,
he will eke the dormer window open a gray crack
in black, he will tell the thrown sparks up there: "God,

if you exist, make me blue, make me
moonlight!" Later, a man, he'll remember this in *Paris
Through The Window:* a figure raises a pyramid
prism, and dazzle breaks in urgent, primary swaths
on the transformed streets ("I was struck by Paris
light as soon as I got off the train. I felt airborne.

Now I began to understand color!"). Color calls him,
the stuttering, play-at-home, herring-monger's son
of Vitebsk. "The cow in our yard, with her milk as white
as snow, the cow who used to
talk to us." Years later she'll appear as the rouge
all-providing beast that straddles the onion-dome roofs

suckling both calf and man (*To Russia,* 1911); the butter
yellow cow, tongue blatant as an oar, who clunks
to the feedpail (*Farmyard,* 1954-62); the cream-and-char
flop-eared face, almost human in knowing
gentleness (*I And The Village,* 1911) that smiles over
a nosegay, against the geometric sky. The sky

calls him. It watches, it gives, it accepts. "And you,
little cow, naked and crucified, you are dreaming
in heaven. The glittering knife has raised you to the skies."
This after a day with his uncle the masterbutcher, the
blade dragged through ropey throat. Years later, (1947), *The
Flayed Ox:* burnt-flesh reds on blue snowfall. Light,

he thinks, is retrieval: it sees, and remembers, and
the lamplustre patterns Vitebsk on his peeling
Paris garret's walls — here, in the paints and crusts
of a wind-whistled room, he can open light's tight
lovers-hug and warm himself by the sparks it never
let go. He reaches up, plucks an image: the Sabbath

candles, flames firm as spearheads, defining the room.
His father, coat soaked in brine, hands
frozen in crystals of herringwater, pulls his own feet
like carts through the flagstone yard and
without resting this one night of the week, washes,
bends his fierce head, dons the prayershawl. Samovar

steam, patchy gray as a headscarf, drapes one corner.
The meanest house, built almost of kindling, still glints
in its cocks' wattles, in a purse's small coughing
a kopeck. The blindman, his house a
sack on back, his eye a stick, floats
through the soapgreen day like a brown cloud. Hassidim

all, and Hassidic possibility: any beggar sawing sweet
plaint on his violin could be an Angel of the Lord, and wing
the goats or horn the starlings. When Mama
Feiga polishes silverware it's a blessing: each prong
so bright, a fork in both hands carried down the dirt street
makes menorah. These

are the shinings he does in
oils now, and will do for sixty years, and in
clays, and in glasses. Vitebsk will fall
whole out of the air in any city, its raggedy skyline
a small gold everyman's crown
floating eyelevel. Paris — there it was the poets

who first understood, and supported, that working
the gleam into shape. So — here, twelve stanzas
for the twelve Jerusalem windows he will stain
in '62. Six lines apiece, for the points in the star
of david. If word and picture can look to mutual
source (and all quotations are from his book

Ma Vie) let his friend the poet
Blaise Cendrars (1887-1961) appraise his calling:
The window is an almanach
Chagall
Chagall
Astride ladders of light

And Dinah, the daughter of Jacob, did walk in the field
And was seized by Shechem, the Prince of that country, and
    was defiled.
Then did her brothers take sword and travel wrathful through
    the knee-high
Grasses to Hamor, the King and Father of Shechem. Her
    brothers, Simeon and Levi.

"We are strangers here, and have tented ourselves on thy land
    in peaceful
Intent. Wherefore this violation, so low and disgraceful?"
"Calm thou thy wrath, and let this blind thee not as a very sty
In thy seeing. For my son Shechem truly loveth thy sister,
    Simeon and Levi.

And he would wed her honorably, and my house shall be thy
    house. And we would
Circumcise our every man in the city of Hamor, to make the
    contract good
In thine eyes, and as a sign of trust to Jacob and all his family.
    Thy
Father hath but to send assent." O a glance passed between
    Simeon and Levi.

And Jacob, who was a goodly one, said, "I am well pleased
And it shall be even as Hamor sayeth." They were circumsised,
Every man of Hamor. The third night, silently, sly,
And in shadow, came Simeon and Levi

Without consent of their father to the gates of Hamor and
    Shechem
And found the townsmen weak and sore, and slew them
One by one in their defenselessness. The black, empty sky
Blazed as torch was set to Hamor straw by Simeon and Levi.

Then did Levi unpen the oxen and asses
And thieve them away through the burning grasses.
While Simeon spoilt the women until he, dry
In his manhood, was sated. Such were Simeon and Levi.

And Hamor was destroyed, down to the centipede and
    chaffinch.
And Jacob said, "Thou hast made of my household a stench
Among the Canaanites and we need flee. Before we leave, I
Curse and scatter the anger, and deceit, of Simeon and Levi,

Who in their wantoness hamstring oxen and rouse
Their lust in vengeance. They are no more part of their
    father's house."
Hamor dwindled to ember, to ash. Then did darkness fall
    upon,
And into, Levi and Simeon.

Her name was Rose. In the album's sepia
keeping, it still is.
Rose Seligman, mother's
mother. Fifteen years now, her body
slotted in the small plot of dirt that's
the Yiddish allotment — whatever
quantum of her spirit passed
through a walkup studio's camerashutter:
remains, and smiles. *Smile,*
click/ ruffles, parasol, a dressup day,
in rented clothing. She was the one
when Albert sulked and wouldn't attend *schul* services
when Albert wouldn't finish his peas
poor Albert little Albert
with the well-spanked tooshie, she was the one:
the tale of the Hassid rabbi who jumped like a bridge of flesh
over his prayerbook, to show how play was also a
devout appreciation; the tale about the Hassid rabbi who wouldn't
finish his peas — I forget the reason,
the clever extenuating circumstances her squinty
haggler's wisdom learned in the refugee streets, but
it suffices to say that petulant rabbi was
honored in the next generation and fully acquitted for harboring
loftier tastes. She'd sweeten the kettle
of tea with a thick tilt of honey for me. She'd say
it vill gets better, no matter. It vill gets better.
She died with her blood in her mouth.

My grandmother who wears whale
My grandmother cheeks rouged in beet borsht
My grandmother cleavage
Soup you can chew you can walk back to Russia
on landbridge of soup like this
Newspaper right to left
small dark letters hunched like peddlers
stories of woe on their backs
The angels
The cousins doing well in Dayton, Ohio
The gray one who died

Grandmother hysterectomy
what's that / hush dear / Grandmother *ach* Grandmother *vayzmere*
Grandmother bible it takes the blows
like black walnut on the livingroom table
This is my Grandmother Rose
Rose Seligman porcelain knick-knacks the bones of her apartment
and steam of chicken its soul
My Grandmother *Shabbos*
My Grandmother buy me an orange drink
Mauve shawl on her head
Buttocks like the overstuffed chair
The cousin with a number on his arm
in blue but his eyes have no color
he left that in Germany
Grandmother sunporch
The overstuffed chair
This is come to America fifteen dollars
a hairpin and a china cup in your one good silk babushka
This is scrub
This is twentyfive floors every night
This is one glass of wine
for the Prophet Elijah
Bless bless
Grandmother sing once a year
Horseradish horseradish
garlic and salt
This is Yiddish
the black workers-boot with its tongue
in the phlegm rolling *ich* rolling *ich*
This is Yiddish
two seraphim, Angel Caress, Angel Curse
her hands flying each with a messge
My Grandmother *shtickeleh halvah*
My Grandmother *bissel tz'drayt*
Grandmother *Mumble-Over-The-Candles*
Potato potato
poppyseed dill
This is Grandmother Life-At-The-Heart-Of-The-Cabbage
The dimestore jewelry
pretty enough for the girl from the fishstore

rhinestone sun rhinestone swollen moon glass ruby
sachet it smells of perch and halibut
Grandmother live upstairs
Grandmother wife of Louie
Grandmother Grandma Rosie
My Grandmother white lace in coffin
The angels
The gray one
The thorn and the velvet
This is Rose this is Rose
a red color
This is
Grandmother Thread-Through-My-Body

The photo: accommodates
her bosomy leaning of
muslin housedress;
accommodates like a window — almost
as if she might nod her head through that
tea-colored 1926 air, and raise
the fixative coating like a pane of glass
to beckon me in. "Come, *ess*" — blurred crooking
of hand in that square — "ve gots fresheleh
strawberries, chust like you like . . ."

Suppose the child's
slinked from bed, through the blankety dark of eight
o'clock sleepytime, slinked from bed
to where the shut door admits
a pencil-thin threshold of fluorescence, and his ear
pressed to the door like a leech
swells all night with the old, familiar voices
carrying new words, strange words, too
bent for meaning . . .   *best this way   with*
Louie now   the undertaker   say Kaddish
till she formed, from their breaths, in black
cast iron and weighed like iron
sky on the room . . .

And in the funereal gloom of farewell
services, a rabbi lit by calculating, stagey candles
talked about her through his clacking
marionette jaw, and what was this
plush-stuffed unduly-coiffed grandmadoll
folded in like the laundry . . .

Then

he will remember
that other black box
she fit her best self into,
the camera, and how she's more
alive there now than here like a bolt of dyed damask,
alive in the day
the lens accepted, and safe there.

He will remember
her dialect
Bible stories: how there was a bad man,
Simeon, who brought darkness
to the land and to those who loved him,
darkness for many days — she didn't say
rape or pillage, but meant them — she said
sometimes it would be dark that way. But
he had a son, named
Zohar, *"radiance."* That was to tell us
how what we cherished most would always be held
dear in brightness, and be of avail
after the long dark. Smile.
Click. He will try to remember it
many times, how
it vill gets better.

". . . accepted a commission for twelve huge stained glass
        windows, one
for each of the Twelve Tribes of Israel. They are,
in order: The Tribe of Reuben, The
Tribe of . . ."

Simeon

          Nocturnal, somber
blue. The sin, the stigma,
of Simeon
shadows the few hurt carnelians
and dwarfed greens swabbed on this landscape,
shadows
with its prevailing blue
stain.
          Even the white
glance of sunlight, all colors, whole,
from outside, worries through
this glass transformed to its most
foreboding
runnel of the spectrum.
                              A darkening
planet turns, like a bad decision
being practiced in some politician's mouth; a
sun like a spider crawls feebly about on its
rays. Some dwindling
foliage; the ramping Horse
of War, its tail a miserable
blue swag in the sky; and
the gutted houses of Hamor, with tempera
of Simeon's blue
semen pooled in the streets.
                              The red
on the doves' wings is blood; their only
song now is red gargling. And the bull, the
small glazed bull, that we want to be
fierce and protective, has burst
wings out of its back and, knowing
these hues of devastation, flies
toward the edge as if for shelter

14

in some other
window's version of letting
in glow.
        An eye,
the Eye of God, in a pyramid-shape
in the lower left blue corner
watches.
        And maybe
it was necessary, that axe
so the kindling could spurt
blue fire, that painful blast
so we could build with
blue rock. In some other, later,
glass window, we may see sun's full
white touch taking this
Simeon-blue up into itself, and giving it
back to us mild
and joyful.
        There . . . the
proud, crowned lion of Judah; the
candelabrum-horned deer of Naphtali;
the cosmic fishes of Zebulun . . .
                          But
now, this window, this
unremitting blue. Simeon,
thou must needs be a lesson.

*

In this we see the mystery of the sacrifice.
The rising smoke kindles the blue light, which then joins itself
to the white light, whereupon the entire candle is wholly kindled,
alight with a single unified flame. As it is the nature
of the blue light to demolish whatever comes into touch with it
from beneath, therefore if the sacrifice be acceptable
and the candle wholly kindled, then "the fire of the Lord descends
and consumes the burnt-offering" and this reveals that
the chain is perfected, for then the blue lights cleaves to the white light
above, while at the same time consuming the fat and flesh
of the burnt-offering beneath; nor can it
consume what is below, except it rise and join itself
to the white light. At such time, peace reigns
in all worlds, and all together form a unity.

— transcribed
verbatim from The Zohar,
"The Book of Radiance,"
a compilation
of Judaic mystical lore
(ca. 1200 Christian Era)

*

"The light of heaven is in these windows
and by this means they are part of the good God."

— Marc Chagall, on his
Jerusalem windows, 1961

16

Red
depth.

*

June, 1952: Chagall at Chartres,
to study its glass's almost
floral taking
in, and photosynthetic processing of,

raw scintilla. Here,
in the nave's west wall, a ruby
quatrefoil and cluster are round
glass petals, blossoming

tactile glory. Henry Adams says ". . . one of the flowers
of architecture which reveals its beauties
slowly without end — so
gorgeous that no earthly majesty could bear comparison

with it, and which no other
heavenly majesty has rivalled." It dates from the same
1200 that, elsewhere, in affinity, nurtured The
Zohar's similar opening

up of how something so distant as sky
can enter, and be entered by, us. It's pressed
between the ethereal pages of sunrise
and sunrise. It's 44 feet in diameter. It's the

Rose

Window. You can't say it's nothing
to do with her — or
that we don't live
where light touches.

*

My Grandmother Smile My Grandmother Click
My Grandmother Rose In The *Yahrtzeit* Candle
*

"Not only my hands
with their colors would direct me in my work, but the
poor hands of my parents and of others and
still others, with their mute lips and their closed eyes,
who gathered and whispered behind me, would
direct me as if they also wished
to take part in my life." — Marc Chagall

In the Simeon window: blue, corpse-cool;
When the rabbi leant over her breast like a ghoul;
In the Simeon part of the neighborhood schul;
Where are you flying to, little winged bull?

*

Where glass is pierced
    without being broken and so
    alleluliahs the virgin birth

Where the Ancient Egyptian Apis-Bull is born
    of a sterile cow's being struck by a ruddy,
    phallic extension of sun

Where "Zeus" is derived from the Indo-European
    dyu, "to shine," and Zoroaster is framed
    in His nimbus, and Ahura Mazda in His halo

Where every stem conducts glory like tungsten
    so every pear is an Edison bulb

Where the lump of coal holds its yellow lick
    waiting inside, like a caged canary
    It won't sing until the black hood is lifted

Where Palomar astronomers fiddle with moon, with stars
    like dials on a radio
    They want to hear The Music of The Spheres

Where it travels, 186,000 mi/sec
    but fits in a leaf
    Where it leaps
    between the herbivore's cells like telegraphy

Where it humbles the President's throne

Where shadowrazor shaves the sundial's face
    Where moon lets her white nylon dangle

Where "comet" is only another name
    for a ruffling hem of the angel's skirts

Where the high, clear
    story of Simeon

Where the high clerestory of Simeon
    testifies: Radiance will be born of tragedy

Where the eye's black mouth sings
    li(gh)tany

Where
    "The mechanical energy of a pea
    falling from a height of one inch, would,
    if transformed
    into light energy and used without loss, be sufficient
    to give a faint impression of light
    to every man who ever lived."
                          — M.H. Perenne,
                  Optics, Painting & Photography

Where we live. Where we live.

20

At the present time, I know of approximately 150 cases of "near-death experiences." What is perhaps the most incredible common element in the accounts I have studied, and is certainly the element which has the most profound effect upon the individual, is the encounter with a very bright light. Most of those who are Christians in training or belief identify the light as Christ and sometimes draw Biblical parallels in support of their interpretation. A Jewish man or woman identified the light as an "angel." A man who had no religious beliefs or training at all prior to his experience simply identified what he saw as "a being of light." The dying person feels completely surrounded by it and taken up in it, completely at ease and accepted.

— arranged from Raymond A. Moody, Jr.'s
Life After Life

*

Smile.

Click.

The Little Boy closed his eyes. What he wanted to see, he kept that way — cached in his head, like the Shinystone wrapped in cloth in the corner of the Toy Chest.

Then he closed his ears, so he couldn't hear Old Gabby Rabbi rattling on about Dust and Giveth And Taketh Away. That wasn't his Grandma anyway, that puppet up there in their wooden Toy Chest, that wouldn't kiss back. That just wasn't her. So he snuck outside, to find her, to tell her how silly this all was, how scarey, and then she'd comfort him: "here, here, *geb* me your *hent.*"

So when they were all busy making monstermasks of their faces, and drooping like rags, he snuck out. Or maybe he closed his eyes, and only snuck out behind his lids — the way the T.V. People played by themselves on their own side, when the screen went blank. But anyway, he left that place. The Little Boy Who Wouldn't Finish His Peas said goodbye to The Gloom Room and stepped outside. It was sunny. Across the road, a field of cows was basking; their shitstink and mamasmell rose in the afternoon breeze like huge tubs of perfume. Here, in the back of the parlor, an unconcerned stream slipped through its thin clay bed. "I wish it could always be this way," The Little Boy said. For the room in the parlor had made him afraid of changes.

"It always will be." It was the Stream. Her voice was low, with small high pockets of sound that rode on top, like bubbles. "Come close, Little Boy." He skipped over. "Pick up that stone there, and drop it in me. That stupid gray one there, that hasn't said an interesting word in a hundred years. Drop him in, right here, and get this kink out of my back."

"Why should I?" For The Little Boy, though he liked the Stream, was peevish.

"If you do, I will tell you something. Only do it right now, and stop saying foolish things, or you shall make the stones feel less stupid than they are. — Ah, good!" The small splash lifted a quick crown of water into the air. The Little Boy sat down, and dabbled a twig in the Stream.

"That was ah, very good, Little Boy, for now an itch in my back has been straightened out. And, oh — do you think it's wrong of me to complain so, and carry a moan in my singing?"

"Why not," said The Little Boy, "if something's wrong?"

"But ah, Little Boy, nothing's wrong. That's what I wanted to tell you. We may want the itch gone, or the heavy boot not to step down, or the rain to keep on playing its hushy lullabye down, but nothing is really right or wrong, or ever disappearing. Do you see?"

"No. This is Dummy Talk."

"Ah, Little Boy, you mustn't say such things. Look, sweet, how my back is straightened. Just yesterday, though you weren't here to see it, though even your Father wasn't here, though the whole City over the hill hadn't hunched a single roof up yet, a bear — there were bears in those yesterdays — rolled a big Rock in part of my back miles off, and I curled like a question mark, many inches out of my course. And tomorrow the banks may pinch my waist, or a huge branch may fall in and make me an outstretched hug for a while, but look, sweet, look how they never make me less or more, but I simply go on and come from, and I always have, and always will, and there's no real change."

"Well you dry up to nothing sometimes. In the summer." He wouldn't be fooled.

"Ah, you're talking like a stone now, Little Boy. And a stone is only Half Right. For it's true I dry up, but I dry up so high, I'm a Cloud. You've seen me, sweet, you've counted those gray ships sailing The Big Blue. I wait there, and

23

there I'm no longer a Stream, but I'm still me, and then when it rains I'm a Stream again. But that's not a change, not really. I've always been me. And when you were a boy . . ."

"But I am a boy," said the Boy. This was Dummy Talk.

". . . A younger boy, sweet, so young that even when you had a long beard and boys of your own, you crawled on your hands and knees and didn't have a house to live in . . . Even then I was still me. At night you'd come with a padding sound to my bank and dip in your shaggy mouth and talk to me of the Caves. How there were long rocks, like teeth, and you lived bundled up in the Earth's warm belly. You would drink me, and I would brush your lips and carry some of you with — but that didn't change us, sweet. We always were. When it thunderstormed I grew wide. And now you've grown wide yourself, in your own way, there are so many little boys. But that doesn't change us, sweet. And later this year I may go to a gray Cloud again. And so may some of your brothers . . ."

". . . But I don't . . ."

". . . and sisters, and in a room somewhere a mother may call her child home and the child may never return. But he's not changed, not really. He may be padding on all fours up to a Cloud, to bend and drink. Do you see? It's true, sweet, come sip me. Here, droop down your head for I love you so."

The Little Boy bent near. He made his lips a pink o. But the Stone said,

"Little Boy, the stream is ancient and wise. You can hear her at night, inside you, when you put your ear to your own wrist. What she tells you then, about the different Towns and Harbors and Beasts In The Sea will be true. So you can be with her that way a while, and needn't drink right now."

"Why not?" For The Little Boy always looked for a chance to Why Not.

"Well the stream is Twice Right. She's right once, when your mother walks out on the back porch and sees you sailing a paper boat and calls in her Ho-Ho Voice, *Little Boy, hello!* And that's correct. And she's right twice, when your mother walks out and sees Clouds being formed in the sky and calls *Oh Little Boy, come in!* but you can't be found, so she falls to the sofa and cries there. And that's correct too, if it happens, but it needn't happen and things would still be once correct and then your mother needn't weep. Do you see, Little Boy? Do you love me?"

"I'm trying. But . . ."

"You can try to be hard, like I am. I don't change, not really, I only stay here, unmoved. Stay with me. Don't go back. Maybe they won't miss you. Maybe they won't weep. Stay with the three of us."

"The *three?*" For The Little Boy had thought the Stream and the Stone his only companions. And then the Light in the air said,

"Little Boy, I've always been here." Her voice was . . . somehow The Little Boy knew that voice. And she said,

"I was there at the start, do you remember, the first two painful kisses driving like spikes in your eyes, the moment they opened? I was there. I never left you, sweet. You thought so, sometimes, didn't you, when they closed the door and clicked off the Smiley Clownlight and then it was Long Lone Darktime, and you. You thought I'd gone away. But I was there, sweet, all around you, you were on the inside of a star, which is dark but is circled on all sides by shining. I was there all along. And you woke in the morning and stretched. I was there. I go a long way, I go all the way around. Right now I'm carrying you, I'm carrying your sight. You're twenty-nine, but I'm carrying How Far You

Can See till you can see how you were five. I know you
don't understand, sweet, hush, it's okay, I'm here high over
the moments that you don't understand. I was always here.
I was there in the faroff Yesterday of Bears, when they
shared the Caves with you, and I'll be here still when the
roofs of the City tumble like a shook House of Cards, I
won't go and I won't let go. Here, give me your hand. Just
lift it up, sweet, put it in mine and I'll walk you back to your
mother and father for now. I remember them too, and I
walked them."

"Aren't you . . ."

"Yes, sweet. I always was, and will be. Here, though, for
now, let's just go back, you and me. I'll walk you. It's such
a nice day out. They love you so."

They saw him walking back to the parlor with one
hand strangely held high above his head.

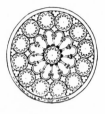

The Family Business

1.

Parents are leaving spaces behind them,
vast exitholes. It's that time
in my generation. And not the empty L
of air on a wheelchair or commode, not the sleeves
in the closet, not the lozengeshape
graves themselves, account for a larger,
conceptual, absence
in the lives of my friends, that follows my friends
for days, vanishes, and then
opens again in the air and is the
window my friends always lean half out of this world from,

my friends write. They've moved,
for the most part — Leo, Paula, Alan, the
rest — you know. Smudged postmarks
collect on my desk, and each its look of an ancient coin
familiar detail's rubbed from.
                              Last night
I drove the old neighborhood, headlights slow and learning
their way like crutches. And under
my hesitant sense of direction, the car-hum
snarled in impatience, the wiring itched to
grease up and go. We're oh so mobile,
aren't we?, Lease-in-hand, Key-in-ignition. In
the Age of Disappearance, moulted feathers tell the
wonders of flight, a sorry handfull. If Leo's
fingerprint still whorled like a sink draining, there
on a basement's porcelain rubble . . . If
Paula's first pair of menses-panties still stank
where she buried them under the backyard laurel in
misdirected shame and stealth . . . These were the motors
that kept a block of middle-class houses alive
for me, though they'd been abandoned
long ago to strangers. Alive! And even so, after
neglect, in the dark those engines
of memory spat and faltered.
                              Strangers

31

— so they called the police. What I said then was
lost and *scouting an address* and
that wasn't so much a lie. What I want to say in
fuller truth to you is: my eyes checking,
doublechecking, my eyes at a window like thumbs
on a luckystone, rubbing,
rubbing, meaning *I know it's still here
and so I'm here,* rubbing for proof.

*

If I had a child
I'd go to his room, right now
at 4 in the morning, and bend
to the little business of oxygen
where his mouth works, just
to make sure
again for my tenth time tonight
that the chemical pawnshop
is open, is making the fair exchange.

*

In the Age of Disappearance, we want
that legendary
mockingbird and chameleon
we could save the world's whole profusion
in, for keeps, and carry.
                              And really, even
that wouldn't do.

Well I have no child. The shingle
& Son is small, and in its pouch. And
having read friends' letters, *negation . . . terrible
vacuum . . . losing hold even of myself,* I could curl
in bed until morning, be my own and only child, make a child's
self-defining gestures — fondling my sex, but
beyond sex. The rub, the
rub all night, to make sure.

2.

Listen: I'm going to tell you
about the relationship between stars and music.

Wail All Night
At THE TAJ MAHOWL!!! Hepcats
do. Grotesque, yes I know, this India oniondome
painted red/white/blue and spotlit
on the shores of Low Pócono Lake. It's also
indigenous, and true. Inside,
the sound of the sax is fuchsia. *Hot* fuchsia.
The band's tuxed — formal bibs, black on white,
like something legally binding. Big Dan's
Big Band, past midnight!, *for YOUR Inka-Dinka-Do-Pleasure.*
Claaass. But A-1 class. The four trumpets move
through air with the intricate pattern and synchronization
of Air Force jets on July 4th. High and
smiley, baby. Put it down plunk on my plate. I mean
smooooooth. The floor's green. The song changes. Then the
floor's amber. Deep, romantic amber and you're
darn tootin'. Everyone's happy, so why do I
have to mention loss? Outside,
                         wind minces the lake.
The lovers make figure elevens
strolling the grounds. Brrr it's cold. Here maybe
my arm will help. The world's this topiary
a gardener let go furzy at the edges. Thanks I
feel better now. A lot. The Nile's not so
mysterious as this, so dark, so complicitous, the
barges cargoing borsht up the Danube somewhere
on the other side of the globe, the jungles of Katmandu
where The Rites of The Tamarisk Moon still take place
Benny told me, aren't so exotic
as Danceland's garden. Far away, the floor's blinking
amber and green like a fruitfly's eyes. But here it's me
and you and the breeze and the sable stole
that used to be Grandma's, and all that

era, or all that era
pertinent to a lineage, radiates
strong from its storage. You're
clearing the attic. They won't need
these now. Your mother's pearls.
Each makes the light round at slightly
a different angle — this necklace, this unintended diagram
of a lunar calendar, sliver to full. Your
father's straw boater. War bonds. The huge cathedral-
fronted radio. The boogey-man glasses
your father put on with the boater, and capered
the frontroom caroling "Crazy Maysie
Kissed The Boys And Whoops-A-Daisie." Of course
you laughed, and mother. It was all he had
to bind with — epoxy, leathertied-eyelet, dowel-and-mortise
clown act. "Hey, champ, how come you can't kill the carpet?"
He was afraid every night "Get *this* — Because
it's already dyed!" of the world, the world

forsaking him, the world with its mad-eyed composer
and musical notation done
in barbed wire; the world with its teeth; with its children
reported missing and maybe the german shepherds would find a
        shoe
by Fall Creek, that's all; the world with its fires; with
bums, with bums who sleep in puke, and any one of them once
had a family, just like yours; with weeping, with barrel-bottom,
terminal ward, the antichrist, diaspora, a single
wrinkle from Great-Grandma's body
you wake to discover has passed overnight down to you

. . . and this is his watch where time went around
like a grist mill, and he was a brave brave man.
All day sorting junk, and it's come to this:
in the album
under the draped Victrola coated by a resiny dust beneath
the attic gable's almost pharaonic
pyramid of calm darkness . . . Flattened, brittle:
the rose. Red flame and green fuse
they touched you off with

under the moon, in the Danceland lagoon. I've
got something for you. *We'll croony-croon-croon.*
Oh, a rose! They're the only couple out
rowing tonight. The sax, though it's muted and far
inshore, still swizzles their bloods
just a little. Sometimes in the history of the sky it
all rests on a flower. *And spoon*
through Jooon! They disappear into each other . . .

We find them.

The night falls quickly,
flat and black
as a 78 from a record changer

dispensing our parents' old
wooing tune . . . and the nebula
the needle spirals in it.

We find the records.
We play them.
Their music like light
from dead stars
still touches us.

3.

"Paco! Pa-a-a-co!"
                    It wafts,
like a magician's pull, yards long, from this four
year old boy and is its own collected
density of air, amid the clouds New Mexico's setting sun brushes
rouge and vermillion. "Pa-a-A-A-a-co!" But magic's only
a being fooled. And this is a fact: the dog's
lost and the night's coming on and the chill's started pinching and

this is the woman who's lost her vision
        A lid closes over an eye like a coffin's
this is the worker who's lost his position
        A spirit goes jelly, a spine softens
this is the wife who's lost her husband
        These are the children she's wadding like tissues
this is the lost war, this the lost homeland
        These are bodies in ashes
this is the raped girl who's lost her reason
        I used to be clean oh I was! was! was!
this is what the world can do

and, given the opportunity,
does.

        And / something like the news story of the guy who
tried to find "the single
true America," couldn't, and so in a way
did/ this is
a little poem
in a large confusion, far past
loss of breath and lost reader, determined to end
on a small, saving, gesture:
                        something
in the way a compassneedle revs up; a
marriage counselor talks his clients, and
talks, and talks, in ever finer-focusing
circles; a Chief of Missing Persons paces
the Bureau's rug, around, around, till he
generates a solution; in the way, almost

magic (yes magic desite the blah-blah all
about wavelengths), Paco
pricks up, gains direction, and follows
home the 50-Cents-High-Above-C-Dogwhistle which
is a shrill beckon now
in his labyrinthine hearing; / something

funnels me back

through the poem's coils: recordwhirl / nebulaspiral / Leo's
fingerprint's spin / the rose
with its eddy of petals, the vortex-rose

funneling me back, and funneling me back:

I'm twenty-nine/ I'm trying to find
location, again, through wordage. For the
nth time tonight I cross out, then rewrite:

I'm seventeen/ In the zealous despair
of the adolescent sex drive, I'm fuck-grinding
into my pillow for comfort, half-remembering
earlier comfort in bed:

I'm four/ I'm sleeping.
I don't know, through
unconsciousness, the special set uncertainty gives
the love on my father's face.
But even through blankness, his
footsteps register.
And I can tell you this:
he stops at my room
for the tenth time this night
and stoops to the small allotment of the night
I push out and take back
and is there.

flag / mole / witch / pygmy / stars / & iran
the connections

*

A mole is shuffling the bones of the dead
buried in my country. His snout is a pink sprout
the texts call *star-nosed,* he sees with what we've turned
into the duller responses of hardon and gooseflesh.
                                                        Now
he's a dark bag of oxygen
in the nun's chest; this is theology. Now
he's all four clawed paws slicing out of a
governor's pelvis; this is history. Now he's nudging
a judge's skull so the dirt in the
bucket of jaw lilts, and if that isn't
muckraking nothing is and
maybe we should try, too, to burrow
our archaeological layers. They're the earthworm's
baklava.
              Here, light rhythm of
arrowheads and minié balls set in a decade's
soil like musical notation; the dead are singing
their anthem. The dead are raising their flag:
white stripes
on black, then a pink star
nosing its way through that ribcage.

*

In Freedom Countie they discovered
"an Witch. She was seen to bee breueyng
a Foule Drynk" /she said "tea
onlie; and an Herb-Butter" /they said
"an Iron untill it bee Whyt Hot to Purify
her Eyes" /she said *Me a*
witch, eh? Then me curse ye, and on the
day me bones rise, Repent Or Else for
that be the doomday me curse works.

Then we moved West. There's a coven
in L.A. — like a pin in the far edge
of an unrolled map of the country, that keeps it
from furling East
into itself again.

*

On the eve of his retirement, my father
darkens all of the house's lights but
one candle, and sits with his moon face
reflecting it fully, all night, the whole
skeletal, fissured, night long, till just the
wane-moon his smile is left
like a chair runner rocking his features
sleepy at last. That smile,

the shit it ate . . . He sold insurance, Hello
Mrs. Kojzki what a nice frock oh and look
how pretty Giselle is. The smile. His little
square of customers The Company sectioned out, each
year smaller, each month ten p.m., every day
three floors up: Hello Mrs. Partolini. The smile, a
rag he buffed his life with. He called it rubbing
shoulders with the world, how you got along,
how you got. And he had his reasons,
okay, I know, the Depression and his own father my
Grandpa Albert blind. The wink the smile. For every
penny a star darkened in the sky and

tonight, on the eve of his retirement, for the
gold watch, the last free star
blinks out. And the few, the bartered stars, that remain
burn the old constellation more clear
than a dictum against this evening's black expanse,
The Kissed Ass, what
we live under.

*

"Xmbert, it's so *bad* here! It's rflepping!"
Ginnie, long distance "lonely" an army base
"and the *creeps*" an *Iranian* army base "drudgery"
teaching Iranian soldiers English "I . . . want . . .
a . . . loaf . . . of . . . bread" She wouldn't
kiss, though it hung in her window all night
like a huge gouda moon, that constellation, Ginnie
wouldn't kiss. "can't win" I don't know a thing
about Iran "if you don't play the game" but picture it
dead, a large dead length of dust and salt formations
with Ginnie going "loaf" *lobe* "no, *loaf,* listen:
l-O-H-f, now you say it" *lobe* Desperation
makes strange jobs "not that I didn't have connections,
I didn't *want* conneczhmp" The transatlantic
cable spasms and tics "My last job, the Academy of
Emorgeflee Pramkits, the day I saw the editor of
Plachpis Review flounce in with this pretty
blowfish on his arm and in the next grepstympish
issue there she is, Albert, with this
terrible poem." I look it up. It's a

terrible poem. And Ginnie's only connection
is terrible, sputtering through the water. "I'm delbmenk!"
And Ginnie isn't pretty, just good. And a
loaf of bread never cost so much. And it's night, at
least I assume it's night for her (here, New York, a
fishbelly light says it's day) and I don't know anything
about Iran, or the Pentagon's plans for Iran, but I
see Ginnie walking its dark salt fields,
the whole country clasped for a cape at her shoulders,
her burly shoulders, her shoulders she wouldn't rub,
let the stars be a rosin tonight. Just once, soft
and accommodating. For her, for someone who didn't
play kiss. I see her out there, telling the sky "loaf,
goddam you, *loaf!*" but it all comes back wrong.

*

The *molimo* pygmies in Africa can't/won't
let their central fire die. Their new village
shapes itself around that fire, another
shared product of it, like heat or glow. A village
lasts half a year though in a sense they're not
nomadic — that is, the fire travels with. Wrapped
in a wax-leaf out of rain and wind, it
folds itself into an ember. And if the fire's the
heart of the village, the ember's its pacemaker
spark. The body rises, packs,
moves through jungle. Alive
in its wax-leaf, the coal keeps the beat.

And I want that burning
hinge-pin for my country, even if
looking at it blinds, even if lifting it
once to put down on this paper
blisters the hands. I want

hissing spat of fat
thieved for a tramp's skillet

soldier's brain beat to a blastingcap of fear
in his chafingdish helmet

perspective drilling the engineer's eye
and the engine drilling mountains

dawn, between the coast
and lowhanging leaden sky, like light
through a lizard's
lid's slit

: a constellation of hard stars
over my country's sleep. In the dark
rainforests, the pygmy elders
stare from their circumference
of fire, into the blackness — they
talk to their fathers. "Hello watching
spirits. We're here at the embers

as you were, we're together, the huts are
threaded with vine and every woman
and man is at the stewpot. This is
good. You made us with your body's seeds
and then we put you in the ground like seeds.
We planted your bones so they could flower
spirits. That was good. Thank you,
good, thank you."

They have a kind of flag they
raise and lower. We'd call it
morning and night.

*

Fifty years later a rare quake
uncovered her bones. Nobody would touch them.
They stayed on the knoll and whistled
wind after midnight.
Ten years after that

every adult male in Freedom Countie
swore off liquor in favor of tea; donated
a tenth-field's share each year to the idiot boy
and cripple-woman; laved salve
on his woman's whipped buttocks; and
bowed his head at the lamb's bleat

when

the mayor, with reliable witnesses,
walking home through the stand of hickory saw
"her bones Rise in the Moonlyte
& Jigg."
(or so the story goes)   /Listen,

it was the mole
exploring under her spine. And we might do well,
too, to rumple the country's backside.

*

And it's so large, this nation, we're
all dwarfs. In Chicago
my father can feel the American night
surround his house as if my family were its
last anther . . . he wants
my sister's body, and mine, to save the world
with Goldbarths. Father,
and fathers, I want to make it good.
I want to say thank you, good, thank you.
I want to use your chipped, yellowed pelvis
for a plow. Second-best won't do: George
Washington's wooden teeth are air now. I want
to dig up your bones, I have to know if they're best
to mourn over, or fertilize with. I'm
confused, I'm tired, I want to work
the sweat in my eye till the sting makes
angels. Lake Michigan grabs
for Chicago's hem every year. The water
is always stropping its waves
on that edge. Though a major airport
can make a man weep and you're small, father,
small, like all of us, I will wrap you
in a wax-leaf when it's time to move on
for someplace better,
and fan you
immense when the work's done.

*

My aunt would read tea leaves.
They'd settle. Once,
from Europe, the entire family

settled. Maybe somebody saw a
brilliant future, I don't know.
Some straight, some stirred, some sweetened.

*

And it's cold tonight, we wish
on a star. A dwarf star.
For the short but
sure luck.

In his own time, in his own country, when the work was
done my father would fall from the world's pincer-tipped
    connections
through the day's last door, his own,
and leave his lips kissed onto his wife's cheek, and rest
on the borsht-red rug or in the gray bath. But
first, every night, a kiss on the doorpost's
time-blackened bar of *mezuzah,* its star's six
points were the real address he drove home to — this as
prescribed by *his* father's father in a more
transcendent land. It was a
kind of cleansing off of the long hours' lies from his mouth
before the pillow
took his face into its dark spaces. / And

in my time it seems important, how
replenishing the homes my friends return to, what
banner above. In my country tonight, the fox cub
is an auburn blur on blackness with loud
henblood smearing the blunt end, and it too will curl
against a mother. A nurse is watching the clock, at a
quarter to three it's a hug. A black whore's
auburn wig rides thousands of bloodcolored rollercoaster cars
of stoplight-glare up its ringlets. When she smacks a certain
latch open she's a mother. The rest falls off with the boa.
Somewhere near Foster a barge's store of oil finds voice
in a moan. Maybe from the oxygen tent a man beneath his aegis,
the clock at a quarter to three, is sitting up, rising
with time's black hand for his last
aware fifteen minutes. So many,
so much . . . There are people I love with slow steps taking them
out of this for a while, to where they can toggle
light on in a room they know, and lay in a lap that out of caring
past sex, makes no demands and asks no questions. / But

52

first it requires their strength to bypass
those other lit windows, a sort of constellation
set in the city's back, that say *it's*
warm in here and so cold outside tonight now
November's a shock in the lungs come
in relax oh and just if you will purse
up and kiss this little
ass at the door and then make yourself comfy

*

Yes the cold frosts
terrible maps, gray
encroachments, up the window. My father
finally goes to bed. In a few more
hours it'll be morning here, Ginnie
can rest in her far Iranian night. His
teeth are false and on the bureau, it's a
way of saving the day's last, only
honest, smile "for Fan and the kids." Ginnie,
he couldn't help it. I love him, his were
different times, different responsibilities. Let the only
ones we can't forgive be ourselves. I know how
hard salt builds, every dawn you wake and Iran's
a mineral taste on your pillow. It's
okay. I promise. What counts — *really* counts —
goes up to ten and we hold our weary faces in them.
Here's the homilies:
Everyone dies and everyone's buried, shoulders
rub world soon enough. Every stone was a star once.
Need isn't want. I promise: I'm
not so cold I'll pucker.

*

So. With a woman, under the fourth
of july night sky, our labor
salting our eyes, and our kisses
leaning on each other for support. My
hand inside her, seeing
by touch like a mole's star. Her
whites streaked bloodshot:
red stripes. So looking up at, and beneath the,
national spangling: *we*
are the flag.

Our hands:
        five points:
                stars:
                        glowing embers.